I0448118

February 2013

SPECTRUM MANAGEMENT

Further Consideration of Options to Improve Receiver Performance Needed

SPECTRUM MANAGEMENT

Further Consideration of Options to Improve Receiver Performance Needed

G A O
Accountability * Integrity * Reliability

Highlights

Highlights of GAO-13-265, a report to congressional committees

Why GAO Did This Study

The growth of commercial wireless-broadband services and government missions, including public safety and defense, has increased demand for radio-frequency spectrum. FCC and NTIA attempt to meet this demand while protecting existing users from harmful interference that can arise as new services and users come on line. To manage harmful interference, FCC and NTIA have historically focused on transmitters—the equipment that emits signals. But, receivers also play a role. Congress and others are considering if further action to improve receiver performance to reduce harmful interference could help enhance spectrum efficiency and meet the growing demand for spectrum.

The Middle Class Tax Relief and Job Creation Act of 2012 directed GAO to study spectrum efficiency and receiver performance; GAO studied four areas related to improving receiver performance, including (1) actions taken by manufacturers and commercial licensees, (2) actions taken by the federal government, (3) challenges, and (4) options identified by stakeholders. GAO reviewed federal regulations and reports prepared by FCC, NTIA, industry stakeholders, and other researchers, and interviewed spectrum users, industry associations, and other stakeholders.

What GAO Recommends

FCC should consider collecting information on the practical effects of options to improve receiver performance. FCC replied that it had initiated such a fact-gathering process; GAO believes FCC's process to date may not provide information on the practical effects of these options.

View GAO-13-265. For more information, contact Mark Goldstein at (202) 512-2834 or goldsteinm@gao.gov.

What GAO Found

Manufacturers and commercial licensees have taken a variety of actions to improve receiver performance. For some services, industry associations—comprised of manufacturers, commercial licensees, and others—have developed voluntary standards that are often used to design and procure receivers, such as those in cell phones and televisions, and to help improve receiver performance. Stakeholders also reported privately negotiating to resolve interference problems and sharing of information as having helped improve receiver performance.

The federal government has used standards and taken other actions to improve receiver performance. Some federal spectrum users, like the Coast Guard and Department of Transportation, have specified or mandated use of industry standards for receivers using certain agency spectrum-based services. The National Telecommunications and Information Administration (NTIA), which manages the federal government's use of spectrum, has also mandated receiver standards for many federal spectrum assignments, such as those for land mobile radios used by emergency responders and radar systems. The Federal Communications Commission (FCC), which manages commercial and other nonfederal spectrum use, believes it lacks general authority to impose receiver standards and rather relies on the marketplace to improve receiver performance. In specific cases, FCC has provided incentives for nonfederal spectrum users to improve receivers. Both NTIA and FCC have taken additional actions to improve receiver performance, like undertaking studies and hosting public workshops.

Although industry and government have taken actions, stakeholders identified three challenges to improving receiver performance:

- *Lack of coordination across industries when developing voluntary standards:* Standards are often developed for a single industry and not coordinated with those using adjacent spectrum.

- *Lack of incentives for manufacturers or spectrum users to incur costs associated with using more robust receivers:* The benefits of improved receiver performance, namely freed-up spectrum for new services and users, often accrue to others and not those incurring the costs to improve receivers.

- *Difficulty accommodating a changing spectrum environment:* When spectrum is repurposed for a new use, upgrading or replacing receivers currently in use to mitigate interference can be difficult and take considerable time.

In addition to greater use of voluntary industry standards, stakeholders GAO interviewed identified several other options to improve receiver performance. For example, interference limits would explicitly set a level of interfering signals that a receiver must tolerate before a user could seek government action to resolve interference problems. Each option entails trade-offs, and many stakeholders noted that a one-size-fits-all solution is likely not desirable or possible. Further, some options, such as interference limits, have not been implemented, and others, such as mandatory standards, have only been implemented for a limited number of users, primarily federal users. Therefore, the practical effects of these options—that is, what would happen if these options were individually or collectively implemented—are not well known, particularly for nonfederal users.

_____ United States Government Accountability Office

Contents

Abbreviations

ANSI	American National Standards Institute
APCO	Association of Public-Safety Communications Officials
ATSC	Advanced Television Systems Committee
AWS	Advanced Wireless Services
CAP	Compliance Assessment Program
CSMAC	Commerce Spectrum Management Advisory Committee
DOD	Department of Defense
FAA	Federal Aviation Administration
FCC	Federal Communications Commission
GHz	gigahertz
GPS	Global Positioning System
IRAC	Interdepartment Radio Advisory Committee
ITS	Institute for Telecommunication Sciences
ITU	International Telecommunication Union
kHz	kilohertz
MHz	megahertz
NASA	National Aeronautics and Space Administration
NOAA	National Oceanic and Atmospheric Administration
NTIA	National Telecommunications and Information Administration
OMB	Office of Management and Budget
OOBE	out-of-band emissions
PCAST	President's Council of Advisors on Science and Technology
PSWN	Public Safety Wireless Network
RTCM	Radio Technical Commission for Maritime Services
SDARS	Satellite Digital Audio Radio Service
TAC	Technological Advisory Council
TIA	Telecommunications Industry Association
TSO	Technical Standard Order
WCS	Wireless Communications Service

This is a work of the U.S. government and is not subject to copyright protection in the United States. The published product may be reproduced and distributed in its entirety without further permission from GAO. However, because this work may contain copyrighted images or other material, permission from the copyright holder may be necessary if you wish to reproduce this material separately.

United States Government Accountability Office
Washington, DC 20548

February 22, 2013

The Honorable John D. Rockefeller IV
Chairman
The Honorable John Thune
Ranking Member
Committee on Commerce, Science,
    and Transportation
United States Senate

The Honorable Fred Upton
Chairman
The Honorable Henry A. Waxman
Ranking Member
Committee on Energy and Commerce
House of Representatives

Radio frequency spectrum is a natural resource used to provide an array of wireless communications services that are critical to the U.S. economy and a variety of government functions, such as national defense, air traffic control, weather forecasting, and public safety.[1] As new spectrum-dependent technologies and services are brought to market in the private sector and government users develop new mission needs, the demand for spectrum continues to increase. A primary driver of the increased demand for spectrum has been the significant growth in commercial wireless-broadband services, including third and fourth generation technologies that are increasingly used with smart phones and tablet computers. Yet, much of the usable spectrum has already been allocated and assigned. Accommodating commercial wireless broadband and unanticipated future services and users, while protecting existing services and users, has proven challenging for the nation's spectrum management agencies—the Federal Communications Commission (FCC) and the

---

[1]The radio frequency spectrum is the part of the natural spectrum of electromagnetic radiation lying between the frequency limits of 3 kilohertz (kHz) and 300 gigahertz (GHz). Radio frequencies are grouped into bands and are measured in units of Hertz, or cycles per second. The term kHz refers to thousands of Hertz, megahertz (MHz) to millions of Hertz, and GHz to billions of Hertz. The Hertz unit of measurement is used to refer to both the quantity of spectrum (such as 500 MHz of spectrum) and the frequency bands (such as the 1710–1755 MHz band).

National Telecommunications and Information Administration (NTIA).[2] For example, LightSquared LLC proposed a nationwide, wireless broadband network that would employ both terrestrial and satellite-based technology. However, NTIA and others identified problems with LightSquared's proposal, including potential interference with Global Positioning System (GPS) receivers which are deployed in a variety of applications, including navigation for commercial and military aircraft.[3]

Concern about interference, such as the potential interference between LightSquared's planned network and GPS receivers, has been a factor in managing spectrum. Historically, FCC and NTIA have used guard bands—idle spectrum that serves as a buffer between systems—and focused on transmitters—the equipment that emits signals, such as television and radio broadcasting—to manage interference between users in adjacent spectrum. However, guard bands occupy valuable spectrum that could be allocated for current and future services and users and transmitters represent only half of a transmission system. The other half of a transmission system is the receiver, and receiver performance, such as a receiver's ability to filter out signals from undesired transmitters, can also affect interference and spectrum efficiency. For example, if receivers, such as receivers in cell phones, do not filter out signals from transmitters in adjacent spectrum, the receivers can be vulnerable to interference, which can inhibit use of adjacent spectrum or require a guard band. Therefore, improved receiver performance can reduce the risk of interference and allow for more intensive and efficient use of spectrum. As a result, Congress and others are considering whether additional federal or industry action to improve receiver performance could help aid spectrum efficiency, among other efforts to make more efficient use of spectrum. In July 2012, the President's Council of Advisors on Science and Technology (PCAST) made several spectrum management findings and recommendations, including that NTIA, in collaboration with FCC, establish spectrum management methodologies that consider both transmitter and receiver characteristics, stating that receiver

---

[2]NTIA is responsible for managing the federal government's use of spectrum while FCC is responsible for managing nonfederal spectrum use.

[3]Because of the unresolved interference problem, FCC prohibited LightSquared from deploying its service commercially. FCC has an open proceeding as LightSquared proposed operating its service in a different frequency band; see *Federal Communications Commission Invites Comments on LightSquared Request to Modify Its ATC Authorization*, 27 FCC Rcd. 14,290 (2012).

characteristics increasingly constrain effective and efficient spectrum use.[4]

The Middle Class Tax Relief and Job Creation Act of 2012 required that we conduct a study of efforts to ensure that transmission systems are designed and operated so as to not compromise reasonable use of adjacent spectrum, with a focus on receiver performance as it relates to increasing the efficient use of spectrum.[5] Consequently, we examined the following questions: (1) What actions have selected manufacturers and commercial licensees taken to improve receiver performance? (2) What actions has the federal government taken to improve receiver performance? (3) What are the challenges, if any, to improving receiver performance? (4) What options have stakeholders and reports identified to improve receiver performance?

To address these questions, we reviewed relevant statutes, regulations, and FCC and NTIA guidance and reports. We also analyzed literature on receiver performance, standards, and interference from academic journals as well as workshop proceedings conducted by FCC, NTIA, and university-affiliated organizations, such as the Silicon Flatirons Center. We interviewed FCC and NTIA officials to learn about actions the spectrum management agencies have taken to improve receiver performance and members of NTIA's Interdepartment Radio Advisory Committee (IRAC)[6] and officials from the National Oceanic and Atmospheric Administration (NOAA) to learn about actions taken by federal spectrum users to improve receiver performance. In addition, we interviewed officials from industry associations representing various spectrum users; commercial licensees and manufacturers; and academics and representatives from research organizations that have participated in proceedings on receiver performance, among other criteria. Through these interviews, we discussed the advantages and disadvantages of improving receiver performance to increase spectrum

---

[4]President's Council of Advisors on Science and Technology, *Report to the President: Realizing the Full Potential of Government-held Spectrum to Spur Economic Growth* (July 2012).

[5]Pub. L. No. 112-96, § 6408, 126 Stat 156, 232 (2012).

[6]IRAC's main function is to assist NTIA in assigning frequencies and in developing policies, procedures, and technical criteria on management and use of spectrum. IRAC is comprised of representatives from 19 federal agencies that use spectrum.

efficiency; actions taken by commercial licensees, manufacturers, and the federal government—both federal spectrum users and spectrum management agencies—to improve receiver performance; and actions that could be taken to improve receiver performance. Finally, we analyzed the actions taken by commercial licensees, manufacturers, and the federal government for a judgmental sample of cases of interference wherein receiver performance played or could play a role. These cases involved (1) interference between cellular and public safety services in the 800 MHz band, (2) potential interference between satellite radio and wireless communication in the 2.3 GHz band, and (3) potential and realized interference with radar systems. We selected these cases to ensure variation in application or use (e.g., cellular telephone, navigation), federal and nonfederal users, and existence of receiver standards, among other characteristics. For more information on our scope and methodology, see appendix I.

We conducted this performance audit from July 2012 to February 2013 in accordance with generally accepted government auditing standards. Those standards require that we plan and perform the audit to obtain sufficient, appropriate evidence to provide a reasonable basis for our findings and conclusions based on our audit objectives. We believe that the evidence obtained provides a reasonable basis for our findings and conclusions based on our audit objectives.

Background

In the United States, responsibility for spectrum management is shared between two federal agencies: FCC, an independent agency, and NTIA, an administration within the Department of Commerce. FCC manages spectrum use for nonfederal users, including commercial, private, and state and local government users. NTIA manages spectrum for federal government users and acts for the President with respect to spectrum management issues. FCC and NTIA, with direction from Congress and the President, jointly determine the amount of spectrum allocated to federal and nonfederal users, including the amount to be shared by federal and nonfederal users.[7] FCC and NTIA manage the radio frequency spectrum in the United States through *allocation* and *assignment*:

---

[7]The Department of State also plays a role in spectrum management by coordinating and mediating the U.S. position and leading the nation's delegation to international conferences on spectrum management.

GAO-13-265 Spectrum Management

- *Allocation* involves segmenting the radio spectrum into bands of frequencies that are designated for use by particular types of radio services or classes of users. (Fig. 1 illustrates examples of services by frequency band.) In addition, spectrum managers specify service rules, which include the technical and operating characteristics of equipment.

- *Assignment*, which occurs after spectrum has been allocated for particular types of services or classes of users, involves providing users, such as commercial entities or government agencies, with a license or authorization to use a specific portion of spectrum. FCC assigns licenses within frequency bands to commercial enterprises, state and local governments, and other entities, while NTIA authorizes spectrum use through frequency assignments to federal agencies.

Figure 1: Examples of Services by Frequency Band

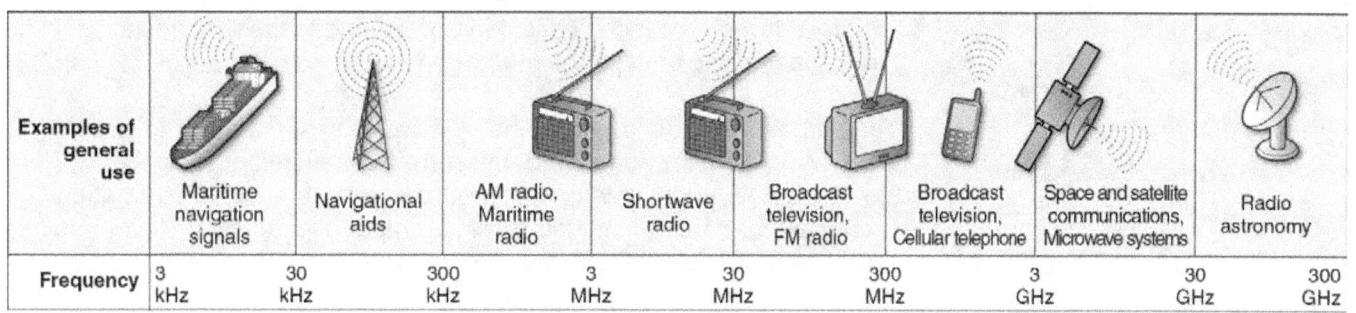

Examples of general use	Maritime navigation signals	Navigational aids	AM radio, Maritime radio	Shortwave radio	Broadcast television, FM radio	Broadcast television, Cellular telephone	Space and satellite communications, Microwave systems	Radio astronomy
Frequency	3 kHz	30 kHz	300 kHz	3 MHz	30 MHz	300 MHz	3 GHz	30 GHz	300 GHz

Source: GAO.

There are several entities that advise FCC and NTIA in their spectrum management activities.

- FCC's Technological Advisory Council (TAC) consists of approximately 50 telecommunications experts that provide technical advice to FCC and make recommendations on the issues and questions presented to it by FCC. TAC is a federal advisory committee organized under the Federal Advisory Committee Act.[8] TAC is currently focused on key issues affecting the deployment of new broadband technologies and services, seeking to spur opportunities for innovation, greater efficiencies, and job creation.

---

[8]Pub. L. No. 92-463, 86 Stat. 770 (1972), codified as amended at 5 U.S.C. App. 2.

- The Commerce Spectrum Management Advisory Committee (CSMAC)—also organized under the Federal Advisory Committee Act—provides advice and recommendations to NTIA on a broad range of issues regarding spectrum management. CSMAC consists of approximately 25 private sector spectrum policy experts that offer insight and perspective on reforms, including long-range spectrum planning. Members are selected based on their technical background and expertise as well as to ensure diversity and balanced viewpoints.

- NTIA's IRAC—an interagency advisory committee—comprised of representatives from 19 federal agencies that use spectrum, was established in 1922 to coordinate federal use of spectrum and provide policy advice on spectrum issues. It was originally organized by federal agencies that were seeking a way to resolve issues related to federal spectrum use in a cooperative manner. IRAC and its subcommittees assist NTIA in assigning frequencies for federal spectrum users and developing and executing policies, programs, procedures, and technical criteria pertaining to the allocation, management, and use of spectrum.

The purpose of a communications system using spectrum is to relay information—audio, visual, and data—from a transmitter to a receiver (see fig. 2). A variety of technical methods exist to encode information such that it can be transmitted as electromagnetic radiation. Antennas are components of both transmitters and receivers used to emit and admit, respectively, electromagnetic radiation-carrying signals.

Figure 2: Components of a Communications System

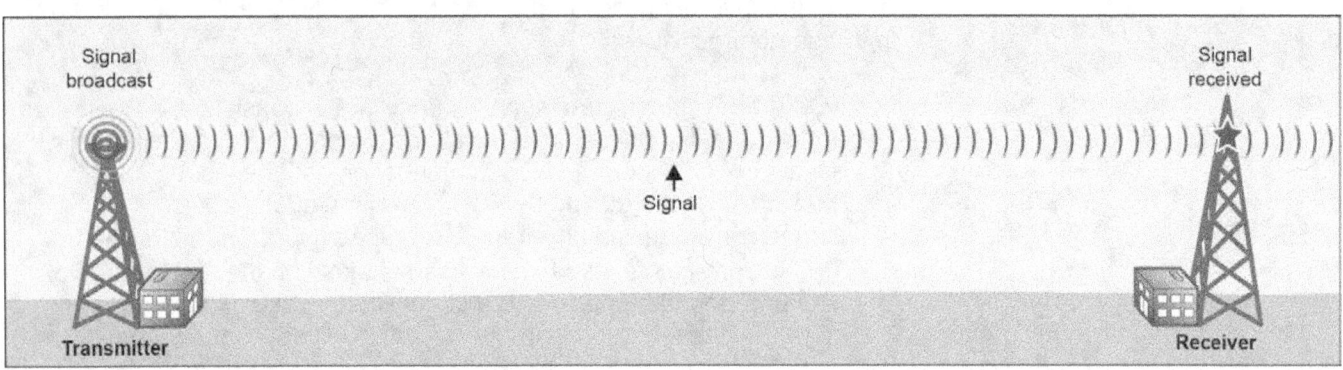

Source: GAO.

A variety of factors influence the ability of a receiver to properly capture the transmitted signal and decode the information for use, including the terrain, distance, and atmospheric conditions between the transmitter and the receiver. For instance, buildings, mountains, and foliage can prevent a transmitted signal from being properly received for some types of communications systems. In other instances, the receiver may be located too far away from the transmitter. In addition, communications systems must operate in environments where a variety of natural and man-made electromagnetic radiation is present. Such undesired radiation could impede a communications system's transmissions from reaching its intended recipients, and such an occurrence is called interference. It is impossible to eliminate all interference from communications systems and not all interference will prevent the proper functioning of a communications system. However, in some cases, the interference is considered harmful, meaning that it "endangers the functioning of a radionavigation service or of other safety services or seriously degrades, obstructs, or repeatedly interrupts a radiocommunication service."[9]

Harmful interference can occur when two communications systems use the same or adjacent frequencies in the same geographic area (see fig. 3). In the first case, co-channel interference occurs when two communications systems operate on the same frequency assignment in the same geographic area. In the second case, adjacent band interference occurs between two communication systems operating on different, but adjacent, frequency assignments in the same geographic area. Adjacent band interference, the focus of this report,[10] has two main causes (see fig. 4):

- Transmitters emit undesired emissions into adjacent frequencies that can cause interference to receivers operating on those assigned frequencies. This is generally known as out-of-band emissions.

---

[9]To be considered harmful interference, the affected system must be operating in accordance with [the International Telecommunication Union (ITU)] Radio Regulations. The ITU is an international organization within the United Nations System where governments and the private sector coordinate global telecom networks and services. 47 C.F.R. § 2.1 and ITU Radio Regulations, Provisions of No. 1.169.

[10]Public Law 112-96 required GAO to study interference between adjacent spectrum uses, rather than co-channel interference between users of the same spectrum.

- Receivers admit undesired emissions from transmitters in adjacent frequencies, causing those receivers to experience interference. In other words, the receiver cannot reject this undesired energy, impairing its use.

Figure 3: Classification of Interference

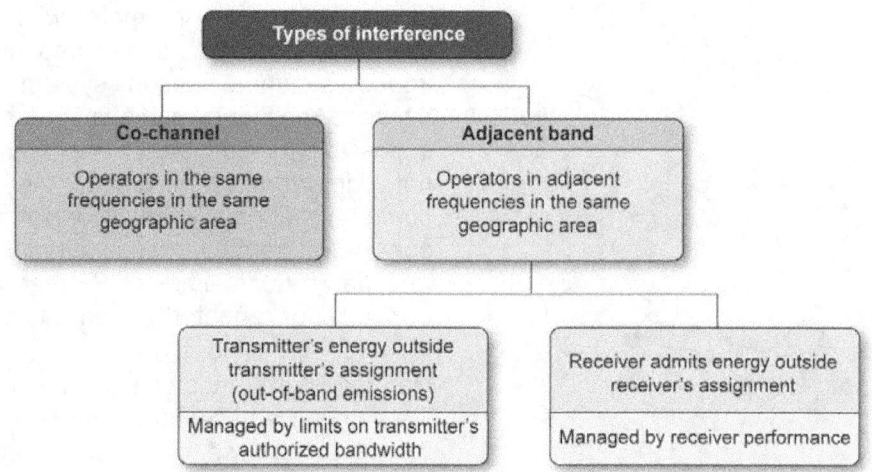

Source: GAO analysis of PCAST information.

GAO-13-265 Spectrum Management

Figure 4: Types of Adjacent Band Interference

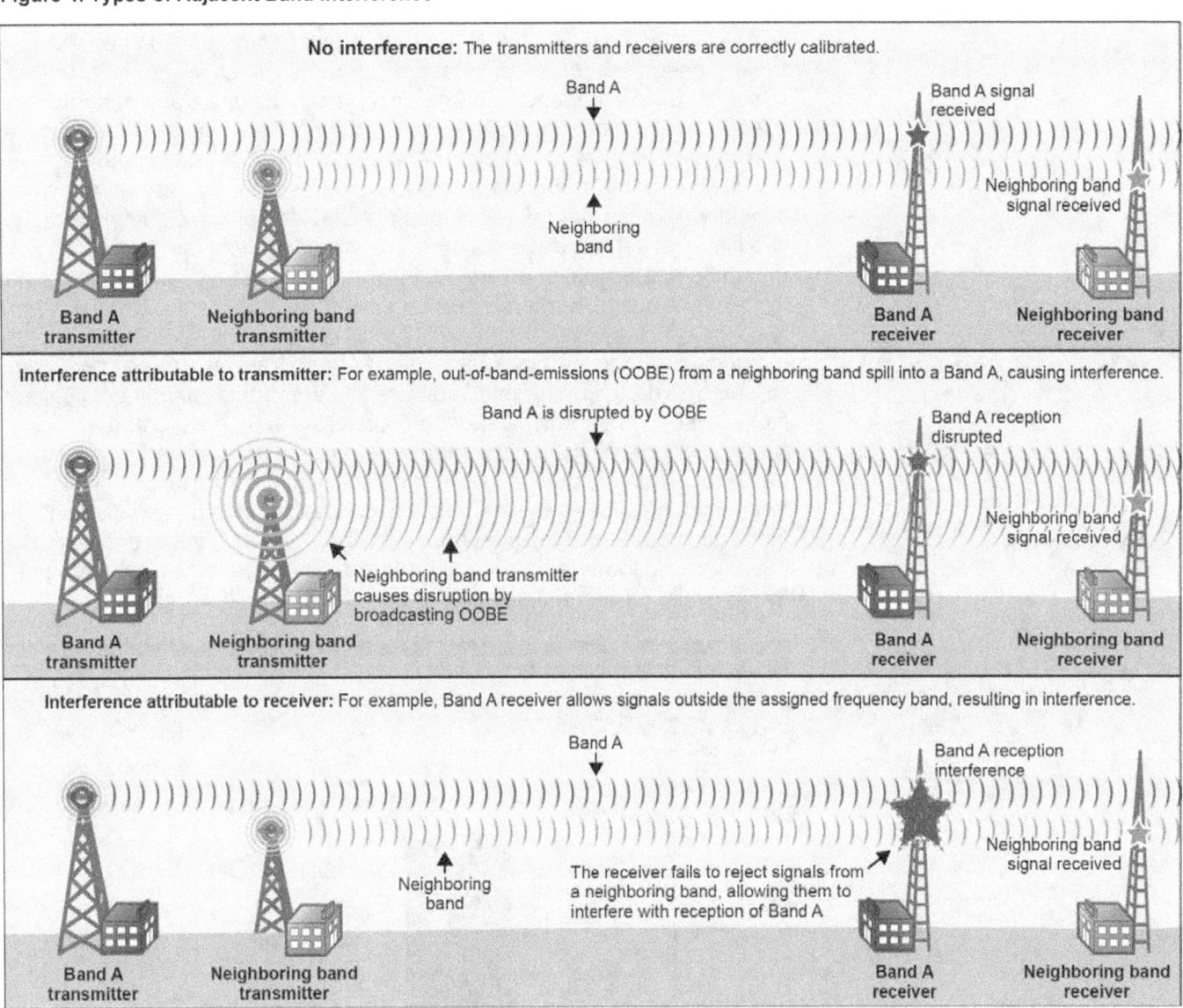

Source: GAO.

Concerns about harmful interference are a factor in FCC and NTIA spectrum management decisions. To prevent harmful interference, FCC and NTIA have primarily focused on setting emission limits on transmitters and establishing guard bands—spectrum that is left unused between different radio services. For instance, FCC and NTIA often place limits on the out-of-band emissions of transmitters to prevent adjacent band interference. In cases where out-of-band emissions cannot be sufficiently lowered, FCC or NTIA establishes guard bands to separate the assigned frequencies of adjacent communications systems. When a spectrum user experiences interference, it can make a claim of harmful interference to the relevant agency—FCC or NTIA—which will investigate and work to resolve the problem. According to FCC, applying the definition of harmful interference often requires case-by-case consideration, as the definition does not provide objective guidance on what level of service degradation or interruption meets the "harmful" threshold and because several factors, including the type and purpose of the service, must be taken into account.

In addition to regulatory actions, well-designed transmitters and receivers can also help prevent harmful interference. Electronic components called filters are used by transmitters and receivers to help ensure that a transmitter only emits electromagnetic signals in its assigned frequency and a receiver only admits electromagnetic signals from its assigned frequency. Ideally, filters would only allow desired signals to pass and block all undesired signals and hence, adjacent band interference would never occur. However, in practice, filters are not perfect, which leads to the potential for harmful adjacent-band interference (see fig. 5).

Figure 5: Perfect and Imperfect Filtering

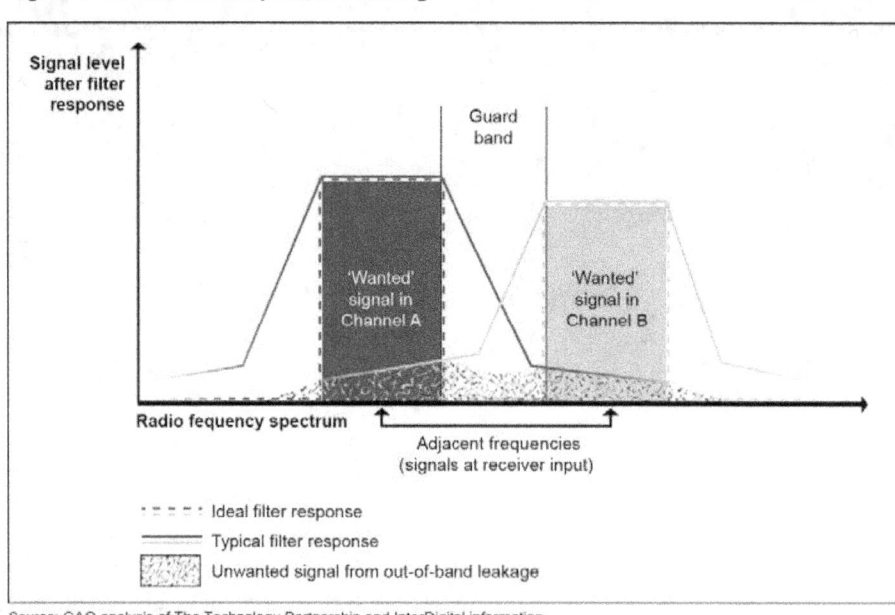

Source: GAO analysis of The Technology Partnership and InterDigital information.

The potential for improving receivers to prevent adjacent-band interference has been receiving increased attention by FCC and NTIA. One of the most recent and high-profile examples, as described earlier, is the potential interference between LightSquared's proposed wireless broadband network and GPS receivers. There have been a limited number of other cases where interference concerns involved receiver performance to date, including potential interference between mobile communications services and satellite radio, comprised of several proceedings over more than 10 years, and between television receivers and unlicensed devices seeking to use spectrum between channels.[11] However, an FCC official stated in a recent testimony that receiver performance is becoming increasingly important as a limiting factor in repurposing spectrum for new uses and in packing services closer together.[12] FCC, working with NTIA, continues its efforts to repurpose spectrum for new uses and technologies—that is, change its rules to reallocate a band of spectrum from an existing use to a new use—to accommodate the growing demand for spectrum.[13]

[11]For a list of situations where receiver performance was a significant issue affecting access to spectrum for new services, including the LightSquared and GPS example, see FCC Technical Advisory Council, Sharing Work Group, "Case Studies: The Role of Receiver Performance in Promoting Efficient Use of the Spectrum," Appendix C in *Spectrum Efficiency Metrics White Paper* (December 2011).

[12]Statement of Ronald T. Repasi, Deputy Chief, Office of Engineering and Technology, Federal Communications Commission, Before the House Communications and Technology Subcommittee, Energy and Commerce Committee, U.S. House of Representatives. "The Role of Receivers in a Spectrum Scarce World." November 29, 2012.

[13]In March 2010, an FCC task force issued the National Broadband Plan which recommended that FCC make 500 MHz of spectrum available for broadband within the next 10 years, and in June 2010, the President issued a memorandum with a similar goal for NTIA working in collaboration with FCC. See Federal Communications Commission, *Connecting America: The National Broadband Plan* (Washington, D.C.: Mar. 16, 2010) and Memorandum for the Heads of Executive Departments and Agencies, *Unleashing the Wireless Broadband Revolution*, 75 Fed. Reg. 38,387 (June 28, 2010).

Selected Manufacturers and Commercial Licensees Have Taken a Variety of Actions to Improve Receiver Performance

To improve receiver performance, manufacturers and commercial licensees have developed voluntary standards that are used to design and procure receiver equipment for some services. Manufacturers and commercials licensees have also used private negotiation, improvements to technology, and information sharing between and among spectrum users to improve receiver performance.

Voluntary Industry Standards

Some industry-led organizations have adopted voluntary standards for receivers.[14] Standards can help guide receiver design to help prevent interference from adjacent spectrum users and can be either voluntary or mandatory. If voluntary, the specific industry members voluntarily agree to meet them, but are not legally required to do so. If mandatory, the standards would have been imposed by governmental action and industry members would be legally required to meet them. Features of receiver standards often include selectivity, the ability of a receiver to separate the wanted from unwanted signals in the adjacent frequency; sensitivity, the detection limit of the receiver to admit the weakest desired signal level; and dynamic range, the range of desired signal levels from the weakest to the strongest that a receiver can admit and function properly. Several industry representatives told us that voluntary standards for receivers adopted by industry-led organizations are working well to limit interference.

---

[14]According to Office of Management and Budget (OMB) guidance, a standard is the common and repeated use of rules, conditions, guidelines, or characteristics for products or related processes and production methods, and related management systems practices. See Office of Management and Budget *Circular A-119*. Pursuant to OMB *Circular A-119*, the term "standard," or "technical standard," as cited in the National Technology Transfer and Advancement Act of 1995, Pub. L. No. 104-113, § 12, 110 Stat. 775 (1995), also encompasses the definition of terms; classification of components; delineation of procedures; specification of dimensions, materials, performance, designs, or operations; measurement of quality and quantity in describing materials, processes, products, systems, services, or practices; test methods and sampling procedures; or descriptions of fit and measurements of size or strength.

Some industry organizations have developed voluntary standards for receivers, including those in the aviation, satellite, and broadcast industries. The processes these organizations use to develop standards are similar and generally include bringing together a diverse group of stakeholders (both commercial and government) for open discussions of specific issues and a transparent, consensus-based decision making process.

- The Telecommunications Industry Association (TIA) is a trade association representing the global-information and communications-technology industry, including equipment manufacturers and commercial licensees, and is an American National Standards Institute (ANSI) accredited standards developing organization.[15] Within TIA, there are committees that set standards for specific spectrum uses, such as the committee that sets standards for land mobile radios used by, among others, public safety agencies. According to TIA officials, developing a new standard includes the coming together of relevant industry stakeholders who have determined that the creation or amendment of standards is necessary, participation by industry and government stakeholders, and a documented, open process. Standards are typically created or amended within 1 to 3 years.[16]

- In the aviation industry, RTCA, Inc. develops minimum performance standards for aviation-related receivers.[17] According to RTCA officials, these standards typically include requirements for rejecting signals from users in adjacent and other bands. Meetings are publicly announced and open to anyone with an interest in the topic or

---

[15]ANSI oversees the creation, promulgation, and use of thousands of norms and guidelines that affect businesses in many sectors. Its mission is to enhance the global competitiveness of U.S. business and the U.S. quality of life by promoting and facilitating voluntary consensus standards and conformity assessment systems. ANSI is also actively engaged in accrediting programs that assess conformance to standards.

[16]When a TIA standard is also an ANSI standard, ANSI reviews the standards-setting process and puts the standard out for public notice, in addition to TIA's steps and processes.

[17]RTCA is a private, not-for-profit corporation that develops consensus-based recommendations on communications, navigation, surveillance, and air traffic management system issues. RTCA standards serve as a partial basis for subsequent FAA regulatory and certification processes.

standard under consideration. The timelines for developing a standard can vary greatly, but typically take 3 to 5 years.

- In the broadcast industry, the Advanced Television Systems Committee (ATSC) has established voluntary industry recommended practices for television receivers, which include requirements for rejecting signals from adjacent spectrum users. ATSC practices are created by a multi-stakeholder group—representing the broadcast, broadcast equipment, motion picture, consumer electronics, computer, cable, satellite, and semiconductor industries—and usually take at least 1 to 2 years to achieve consensus.

Once developed, voluntary industry standards may be used by manufacturers and commercial licensees to design and procure equipment. Representatives of the cellular industry told us that their industry relies on a voluntary approach to receiver standards and receiver performance, pointing out that voluntary industry standards are used on a daily basis between handset manufacturers and wireless companies. Officials at the National Public Safety Telecommunications Council said that the TIA standards for land mobile radios are commonly referenced by public safety agencies when procuring equipment, including receivers. Representatives of two different land mobile radio manufacturers told us that standards form a baseline for performance and that their receivers typically exceed the relevant performance standards.

When procuring equipment, compliance and certification processes can be used to assure users that equipment meets the voluntary industry standards. In some cases, there is a general certification program that covers a particular service. For example, the National Institute of Standards and Technology—in partnership with other industry representatives, the public safety community, and other government agencies—has a testing process for public-safety land mobile radios.[18] In other cases, compliance testing might be carried out by those purchasing the equipment. For example, TIA representatives told us that many of

---

[18]The Project 25 Compliance Assessment Program (CAP) is a voluntary program that allows public safety equipment suppliers to formally demonstrate their products' compliance with a select group of requirements by testing them in recognized labs. CAP is a partnership of the Public Safety Communications Research program, the National Institute of Standards and Technology, the Department of Homeland Security, industry, and the public safety community.

TIA's member companies are involved in testing equipment against standards, although TIA is not itself involved in the certification process.

Negotiation, Improvements to Technology, and Information Sharing

Negotiation. In addition to developing and using voluntary industry standards, some manufacturers and commercial licensees privately negotiate interference concerns. Representatives of the cellular industry told us that their industry deals with interference on a daily basis, as interference problems are increasing and have become a regular part of doing business. Several industry representatives highlighted the cellular industry as a sector in which the wireless companies and manufacturers work in concert to maximize efficiency; these efforts often occur within the cellular spectrum bands and among like services. According to one industry representative, voluntary negotiations helped resolve interference to fixed microwave services that occurred in the past.[19] The interference occurred when a new service began operating next to a microwave service in the 1.9 GHz band, where the microwave receivers had been in operation for 30 years. To resolve the interference, the parties discussed whether to add filters to the transmitters or the receivers and decided to add filters to the receivers.

Improvements to Technology. Some manufacturers and commercial licensees also apply technological advancements to receivers and their components to improve the performance of receivers. For example, RTCA representatives told us that advances in filtering technology have been utilized in modern aviation equipment to reduce interference. One manufacturer of land mobile radios told us the company is continually making changes to equipment to improve performance and reduce interference. During the discussions to resolve interference to public safety operations using land mobile radios in the 800 MHz band, this manufacturer examined technical advances in receiver design that could help alleviate the interference.

Information Sharing. Some manufacturers and commercial licensees share information to help improve receiver performance. The creation of standards, discussed earlier, is one area where manufacturers and

---

[19]Fixed point-to-point microwave service refers to a radio communication between two fixed points, such as between two stationary cell phone towers. These connections, known as links, are used for a variety of purposes, including connecting cellular sites to the telephone network and relaying television signals.

commercial licensees, as well as other stakeholders, share information for the purpose of improving receiver performance. One equipment manufacturer told us that bringing together different stakeholders brings forth the best ideas to solve problems. Another example of communication helping to improve receiver performance was the sharing of information by commercial licensees, manufacturers, and industry associations to create guidance in response to interference between cellular and public safety services in the 800 MHz band. In this instance, after reports of interference were made in a number of locations, representatives of the public safety community and the wireless company involved came together to help resolve the interference. An equipment manufacturer said that there was a lot of cooperation and coordination among the stakeholders as they wanted to quickly eliminate the interference adversely affecting the mission-critical communications of public safety agencies using land mobile radios. As a result of this coordination and information sharing, a Best Practices Guide was created that contained information on how to prevent interference and mitigate existing interference.[20]

The Federal Government Has Used Standards, Procurement, and Other Actions to Improve Receiver Performance

To improve receiver performance, federal spectrum users have mandated use of industry standards for receivers, specified system requirements to procure equipment, and negotiated with other spectrum users to resolve interference concerns. NTIA has mandated the use of standards for many federal spectrum users while FCC has not done so for nonfederal spectrum users, but both spectrum management agencies have taken actions to resolve specific cases of interference and conducted research to improve receiver performance.

---

[20]A group including Motorola, the Association of Public-Safety Communications Officials (APCO), Nextel Communications, CTIA, and the Public Safety Wireless Network (PSWN) developed the guide. See *Avoiding Interference Between Public Safety Wireless Communications Systems and Commercial Wireless Communications Systems at 800 MHz, A Best Practices Guide* (December 2000).

Federal Spectrum User Actions

Some federal spectrum users have specified, and in some cases mandated, standards for receiver performance that are often based on industry-developed standards.[21] Federal agencies use spectrum to operate systems both for internal use and for external use by other parties. For external systems, federal agencies can mandate standards that parties must meet to use the system. For example, the Department of Transportation uses ASTM International standards for emerging communication applications among vehicles and roadside equipment to enable safety, mobility, and environmental benefits.[22] Similarly, the Federal Aviation Administration (FAA) publishes Technical Standard Orders (TSO) for communication and navigation systems that incorporate by reference RTCA standards for aviation receivers.[23] According to RTCA officials, compliance with TSOs can be used as one basis for FAA certification of communications, navigation, and surveillance equipment. RTCA standards for receivers typically include requirements for rejecting signals from adjacent and other bands to limit interference.

In addition to using existing industry-developed standards, federal spectrum users work with standards-setting bodies and other organizations to create standards in response to particular cases of or concerns about interference. For example, the Coast Guard worked with a standards-setting body—the Radio Technical Commission for Maritime Services (RTCM)—to create new standards for receivers when its marine radio system—used for applications such as distress calls and port navigation—experienced interference from neighboring services that were

---

[21]In general, these mandated standards are more stringent than requirements for federal spectrum users set by NTIA, discussed in the section below.

[22]ASTM International is a standards-setting body that develops voluntary, consensus-based standards covering a range of engineering disciplines including aerospace, industrial, mechanical, and solar engineering.

[23]For example, RTCA/DO-229D, *Minimum Operational Performance Standards for Global Positioning System/Wide Area Augmentation System Airborne Equipment*, dated December 13, 2006, Section 2, is incorporated by reference in *Stand-Alone Airborne Navigation Equipment Using the Global Positioning System Augmented by the Satellite Based Augmentation System*, TSO-C146c, 2 (2008), except as modified in appendix 1 of the TSO.

operating in compliance with federal rules for transmitters.[24] According to one Coast Guard official, the standards were created in a few months and equipment manufacturers began producing receivers that met the new standards in 1 to 2 years. Similarly, the National Aeronautics and Space Administration (NASA) is currently working with other space-faring nations to create standards to help maintain the spectrum performance of highly sensitive satellite downlink receivers used to obtain data from interplanetary spacecraft missions (e.g., Mars exploration rovers). One NASA official said that adjacent band interference is a concern given the sensitive natures of these receivers and that both transmitter and receiver standards can help to address a majority of interference problems.

When procuring equipment, federal spectrum users also specify system and component requirements, including those for receiver performance. The Department of Defense (DOD) uses acquisition guidance that emphasizes the need to address the potential for adjacent-channel and adjacent-band interference when designing and procuring equipment. As part of this guidance, DOD has established receiver performance requirements that apply to all procurements by military departments.[25] NOAA also specifies system performance, including receiver performance, when procuring equipment. According to NOAA officials, the agency defines a system's expected availability—that is, the time that a system or equipment is capable of being used—when procuring equipment, which is then used to determine specifications for system components and subcomponents including receivers.

Federal spectrum users also privately negotiate with other spectrum users, both federal and nonfederal, to resolve interference concerns

---

[24]In investigating this interference, NTIA reported that the neighboring nonfederal services were operating in compliance with FCC rules and regulations for their transmitters, making it difficult to impose operating restrictions on the operators. Therefore, NTIA reported that practical solutions to solve the interference were to continue to develop receiver standards through RTCM, encourage mariners to use radios that are more resistant to interference, and to develop guidelines for future deployment of neighboring services to reduce interference. See NTIA-99-362, *Evaluation of Marine VHF Radios: Performance in the Savannah, Ga. and New Orleans, La. Port Areas* (Washington, D.C.: March 1999) and NTIA-99-363, *Evaluation of Marine VHF Radios: Compliance to IEC Receiver Standards* (Washington, D.C.: October 1999).

[25]The requirements are included in DOD MIL-HDBK-237D, *Electromagnetic Environmental Effects and Spectrum Certification Guidance for the Acquisition Process* and DOD MIL STD 461F, *Requirements for the Control of Electromagnetic Interference Characteristics of Subsystems and Equipment*, among other documents.

between adjacent spectrum users. According to NTIA officials and IRAC members, interference cases are handled on a case-by-case basis, which can result in making changes to individual systems such as adding filters to transmitters or receivers. For example, a National Science Foundation official said the agency is currently working to resolve interference to receivers that collect and process satellite signals from a nearby TV transmitter that was operating in compliance with FCC rules.[26] IRAC members said that negotiation among federal spectrum users is aided by access to NTIA's database on federal spectrum use and by each agency having a designated spectrum manager. NTIA officials told us that most cases of harmful interference involving federal spectrum users are resolved between the cognizant parties rather than through NTIA.

Spectrum Management Agency Actions

NTIA has mandated the use of standards for receiver performance for many federal users. NTIA sets mandatory standards for federal spectrum users in its Manual of Regulations and Procedures for Federal Radio Frequency Management. According to NTIA officials, these mandatory standards for receivers apply to about 60 percent of federal spectrum assignments, including land mobile radio, fixed, radar, and aeronautical mobile telemetry systems, and additional mandatory standards set by federal spectrum users like FAA cover another 10 percent of federal spectrum assignments. NTIA and federal spectrum users adopt industry-developed standards when they are available for a given service.[27] For federal spectrum uses that have very specific applications or lack a commercial equivalent, NTIA can establish its own standards, as it did for radar systems, or choose to not establish standards.[28] NTIA's mandatory standards, whether set from industry standards or established by NTIA, are used to certify federal equipment, and when procuring equipment,

---

[26]While the parties work to find a solution to the interference, which could include getting a new frequency assignment for the TV transmitter from FCC, the TV operator turned off the transmitter.

[27]OMB *Circular A-119* directs agencies to use voluntary consensus standards in lieu of government-unique standards except where inconsistent with law or otherwise impractical.

[28]NTIA officials said that the federal systems not currently covered by receiver standards are specialized systems operated for scientific and military purposes; for these applications, developing a standard is not practicable because only a limited number of systems are typically manufactured. In cases where there are not standards, NTIA officials said the agency assumes that federal users of spectrum will work out solutions to interference problems among themselves.

federal spectrum users must set specifications that comply with the NTIA mandatory standards. NTIA has reported that these mandated standards have done much to prevent interference to federal spectrum users and that mandated standards establish a baseline of performance but do not prevent users from moving to more efficient or better receivers.[29]

FCC has not set mandatory receiver standards for nonfederal spectrum users. FCC has specific statutory authority to establish minimum performance standards for home electronic equipment, like televisions,[30] but FCC officials said that the Commission lacks direct authority to impose regulations governing receiver performance in other cases outside home electronics. Therefore, FCC has generally relied on the marketplace to incentivize nonfederal licensees and manufacturers to produce receivers that can reject unwanted signals and limit interference. As noted in the previous section, manufacturers and commercial licensees have taken actions such as adopting industry standards to improve receiver performance. While FCC has generally relied on the marketplace to improve receiver performance, it has provided incentives to spectrum users to do so in specific cases. For example, FCC defined the minimum levels of performance that a receiver must meet to make a claim of harmful interference in the 800 MHz band. Specifically, FCC set minimum levels for receiver performance for non-cellular systems, primarily public safety radios, as part of the reconfiguration of the 800 MHz band to mitigate interference between non-cellular and cellular systems.[31] Therefore, spectrum users that choose to use receivers that do not meet the minimum levels are not entitled to full protection from interference. The public safety community and manufacturers recommended that FCC set objective criteria to qualify for interference protection. In this case, FCC reported that taking further action to improve receiver performance, like requiring public safety radios to fully comply with industry standards to claim harmful interference, would impose costs that outweighed the resulting interference protection.

---

[29]*NTIA Comments on Interference Immunity Performance Specifications for Radio Receivers* (Washington, D.C.: Nov. 12, 2003).

[30]47 U.S.C. § 302a(a)(2).

[31]Reconfiguration involved separating previously interwoven cellular and non-cellular licenses into separate parts of the band. See *In the Matter of Improving Public Safety Communications in the 800 MHz band*, 19 FCC Rcd. 14,969, 15,024, 15,027, 15,029 (2004).

FCC and NTIA have also taken specific actions in response to cases of interference involving receiver performance. FCC and NTIA officials said that interference cases, both potential and realized, are generally handled on a case-by-case basis, so actions are taken that address the particulars of each case. In rulemakings for new services, FCC often invites comment about any receiver characteristics that should be taken into account, particularly for receivers currently in use in adjacent bands. In some cases, FCC has required that a new spectrum user protect the incumbent services in the adjacent band from harmful interference regardless of the performance of the receivers in use, a policy known as "first-in-time rights." The Advanced Wireless Services (AWS)-1 spectrum, for example, was reallocated for flexible fixed or mobile service, such as voice and data content, which raised concerns about potential interference with incumbent licensees in the adjacent band used for broadcast auxiliary services.[32] The new AWS-1 licensee purchased and arranged for the installation of new filters for the incumbent's receivers to avoid causing harmful interference as required by FCC rules for AWS-1 spectrum. NTIA's Institute for Telecommunication Sciences (ITS) investigates cases of potential or realized interference and identifies strategies to mitigate interference. ITS officials told us that ITS tends to work on interference cases that are particularly complicated or difficult to remedy rather than on more general interference or receiver concerns. For example, ITS investigated interference to fixed-satellite service (space-to-earth) stations in the 4 GHz band from radar systems operating in the adjacent band. The ITS report identified the source of the interference, in this case primarily because of poor filtering, and listed various solutions to remedy the interference. Moreover, NTIA is currently leading an interagency working group to examine receiver performance standards for GPS devices for federal users and the feasibility of accommodating terrestrial broadband systems in the bands adjacent to GPS. However, based on a 2011 Silicon Flatirons Center workshop of experts from government, industry, and academia, one theme drawn from reviewing case studies of adjacent band interference was that information can be lost when interference problems are resolved on a case-by-case

---

[32]AWS is the collective term used for new and innovative fixed and mobile terrestrial wireless applications including those using voice and data content, such as Internet browsing, message services, and full-motion video. Broadcast auxiliary service is primarily used for electronic news gathering to distribute live television shots from the field to the studio.

basis, as other operators with similar problems might not have access to the resolution of other cases.[33]

In addition to mandatory standards and case-by-case actions, NTIA and FCC have completed reports, requested research, held workshops, and taken other actions on receiver performance.

- *Reports.* NTIA's reports on the topic include a 2003 report summarizing existing receiver standards, both voluntary and mandatory, established by federal agencies, industry associations, and international groups, and a 2005 report compiling existing interference protection criteria for various radio services used by the federal government.[34]

- *Requested research by federal advisory committees.* In 2010, NTIA's CSMAC studied interference and dynamic spectrum access that resulted in recommendations on guard bands, equipment standards, and enforcement aimed primarily at NTIA and federal spectrum users.[35] In 2012, FCC's TAC studied receivers and spectrum and presented recommendations to FCC.[36]

- *Public notices and workshops.* FCC has taken steps to seek stakeholder input and encourage dialogue on receiver performance though public notices and workshops on receivers and spectrum efficiency. In 2003, FCC issued a Notice of Inquiry seeking public

---

[33]Madelaine Maior, *Efficient Interference Management: Regulation, Receivers, and Rights Enforcement,* A report on a Silicon Flatirons Summit, held 18 October 2011 (January 10, 2012).

[34]NTIA Report 03-404, *Receiver Spectrum Standards: Phase 1–Summary of Research into Existing Standards* (Washington, D.C.: November 2003) and NTIA Report 05-432, *Interference Protection Criteria: Phase 1–Compilation from Existing Sources* (Washington, D.C.: October 2005). The 2003 report summarized NTIA's review of existing standards and has not been updated since that time.

[35]Dynamic spectrum access technology enables systems to actively search for unused spectrum and organize a network of transmitters and receivers to operate in it, thereby ensuring that no interference is caused to other users. Dynamic spectrum access technologies are currently able to sense for available frequencies before transmission (listen before talk), but not sense during transmission (listen while talk) which could allow more seamless communication while moving between spectrum bands.

[36]The findings and recommendations from these advisory committees are described in greater detail in the last section of this report on options to improve receiver performance.

input on whether and how it should incorporate receiver performance specifications into its spectrum policy.[37] Stakeholders submitted comments that varied in their support for greater action, whether taken by FCC or the market, though a majority of comments favored a market driven approach, like voluntary industry standards for receivers. In 2007, FCC closed the proceeding stating that action did not appear to be needed at that time; FCC officials said that the comments from the rulemaking presented no clear solution, particularly as no single solution fit all interference problems.[38] More recently, FCC held a 2-day workshop in March 2012 dedicated to spectrum efficiency and receivers. Participants, including licensees, federal agencies, equipment manufacturers, and component providers, examined the characteristics of receivers and how their performance can affect the efficient use of spectrum and opportunities for the creation of new services. Most participants in the workshop's concluding panel, which was comprised of a mix of stakeholders, noted that the status quo, as it relates to receiver performance, was not sustainable and that further action is needed.

Several Challenges Impede Further Improvements to Receiver Performance

Although manufacturers, commercial licensees, and the federal government have taken steps to improve receiver performance, many of those with whom we spoke commented on what they perceive to be the challenges to further improvements. These challenges include the lack of coordination across industries when developing receiver standards, the lack of incentives to improve receivers, and the difficulty accommodating a changing spectrum environment.

---

[37]This Notice built off the work of the Spectrum Policy Task Force, established by the FCC Chairman in June 2002 to assist FCC in identifying and evaluating changes in spectrum policy that could increase the public benefits derived from the use of radio spectrum. In 2002, the Spectrum Policy Task Force Report recommended that FCC consider applying receiver performance requirements, through incentives, regulatory mandates, or some combination both, to facilitate greater access to spectrum. Spectrum Policy Task Force Report, ET Docket No. 02-135, 35, p.31 (November 2002). See also *In the Matter of Interference Immunity Performance Specifications for Radio Receivers, Notice of Inquiry,* 22 FCC Rcd. 8,941 (2007), and Review of the Commission's Rules and Policies Affecting the Conversation to Digital Television, 18 FCC Rcd. 6,039 (2003).

[38]In closing the proceeding, FCC noted that it could address receiver performance problems in individual future proceedings for specific services or frequencies.

Lack of Coordination among Those Developing Standards

Standards are often developed for a single industry operating within a defined area of spectrum, such as the cellular industry. While members of a particular industry coordinate with each other, they may have little or no communication with services operating in adjacent spectrum bands. Although standards-setting bodies have published receiver standards for many services, FCC officials and several other stakeholders we interviewed told us that standards are often not developed in coordination with stakeholders representing adjacent services. For example, some aviation equipment operates in the frequencies above the FM radio band. The aviation community sets its own standards, while the FM radio community develops its own standards. Each group has its own representatives who communicate within their own industry but not with those in the other industry. This lack of coordination and lack of information sharing means that the impact of standards set by one group upon other groups is not always assessed, and immunity to adjacent-band interference is not necessarily addressed.

There is also no publicly available compendium of current receiver performance standards or specifications to facilitate coordination or understanding across spectrum uses. FCC officials explained that while receiver performance standards have been developed for some services, there is no catalog of these standards, making it difficult to locate this information. FCC officials also told us that information about actual receiver performance is not readily available. Typically, this information only surfaces in the context of a rulemaking. For example, FCC made requests to equipment manufacturers for information about their receivers and was told by several that the information was proprietary, as companies did not want competitors to acquire information about signal strength or the energy level of devices, among other information.

In addition, since standards are largely voluntary for commercial users, the extent that industry standards are used remains unknown. In fact, just because voluntary standards exist does not mean that licensees and manufacturers will use them. For example, with regard to the recommended practices for the manufacture of television sets, it is not known whether all manufacturers adhere to the recommended practices since the practices are voluntary and television licensees that broadcast television signals do not manufacture television sets or specify their operating characteristics—a situation known as *decoupled receivers*.[39]

Lack of Incentives to Improve Receivers

A lack of incentives for spectrum users and equipment manufacturers to improve receiver performance was another challenge that many industry associations and other stakeholders we interviewed cited. As one industry researcher explained, there are no incentives for manufacturers to build more robust receivers, primarily because the manufacturers will not receive the benefits. Rather, those who want to make more spectrum available or share spectrum will benefit. One industry representative stated that the real question is one of motivation. Improved receiver performance to limit adjacent band interference often requires the addition of filters and can increase the size, weight, power consumption, and cost of the receiver. Additionally, there is no business case that can explain why a business would accept these downsides so that others can benefit when implementing a new system in an adjacent band. Another industry representative echoed that position and told us that, independently, the private sector has no motivation to spend its time and resources to protect spectrum for other users, allow enhancements to other services, or accommodate new entrants. Instead, as one stakeholder commented, companies have an incentive to make the cheapest receiver possible—that is, a receiver with poor filtering capabilities that is more sensitive to emissions from other bands—and no incentive to work with licensees in neighboring spectrum bands.

Similar to commercial users, federal users also lack incentives to improve receiver performance. The PCAST report stated that federal users currently have no incentive to improve the efficiency with which they use their own spectrum allocation, nor does the federal system as a whole have incentives to improve its overall efficiency. Further, we have previously reported that federal users often use proven, older technologies that were designed to meet a specific mission and may be less efficient than more modern systems.[40] NTIA's CSMAC also recently

---

[39]In general, *decoupled receivers* are receivers that are not controlled by the license holder that transmits signals for a service. Common examples of decoupled receivers include radios, televisions, and GPS devices.

[40]See GAO, *Spectrum Management: Incentives, Opportunities, and Testing Needed to Enhance Spectrum Sharing*, GAO-13-7 (Washington, D.C.: November 2012).

recommended that the federal government, including NTIA, consider incentives, rules, and policies to, among other things, improve the capability of receiving devices to reject adjacent channel interference.[41]

Lastly, the use of private negotiation, which has been used regularly to resolve interference within the cellular industry, can be difficult in cases where there are dissimilar services or many parties. When disputes involve similar services in the same band, operators have similar incentives that facilitate private dispute resolution. This may not be the case when licensees with different services or in adjacent bands are involved. Also, when the number of users is relatively small, negotiation between parties may be able to resolve the problem. However, when there are many users involved, the transaction costs may be prohibitively high. For example, for services where receivers are decoupled from licensees, as in the case of television, the large number of receivers and potential lack of coordination among individual parties makes private negotiation a less feasible option.

Difficulty Accommodating a Changing Spectrum Environment

Stakeholders we interviewed cited accommodating changes to the spectrum environment as a challenge to improving receiver performance. As FCC attempts to accommodate new services and users, the Commission often alters how licensees can use spectrum bands. This repurposing of spectrum, either from a prior use or from no use, often gives rise to concerns over interference, concerns that involve receiver performance because incumbent services have manufactured receivers to operate without interference problems in the current environment. However, if that environment changes, receivers currently in use may experience increased interference. This was the case in the 2.3 GHz band, where interference concerns arose between two different services—Wireless Communications Service (WCS) and Satellite Digital Audio Radio Service (SDARS)—allocated to adjacent spectrum. Although the WCS allocation allowed for mobile service, the rules limiting out-of-band emissions for transmitters made mobile service impractical. After years of attempting unsuccessfully to deploy a mobile service, the WCS licensees petitioned for rule changes. In considering the WCS licensees petition, the performance of the SDARS receivers was one of the critical

---

[41]See Commerce Spectrum Management Advisory Committee, *Interference and Dynamic Spectrum Access Subcommittee Final Report* (Washington, D.C.: Nov. 8, 2010).

areas of contention. SDARS receivers were not capable of filtering out stronger signals in adjacent spectrum. These receiver concerns required technical rules that effectively created guard bands on each sides of the SDARS spectrum to prevent interference.[42]

Innovation on the part of current spectrum users is another factor that can change the spectrum environment. Current spectrum users may decide to make changes to the configuration of their system based on business needs. Such changes can result in interference to adjacent spectrum holders. For example, both Nextel, a cellular provider, and public safety agencies had licenses to operate in the 800 MHz band. Nextel decided to convert its mobile radio architecture from one that used high antenna sites atop buildings or towers to one that used a short-range cellular architecture with low antenna sites to provide more capacity in crowded urban areas. Even though Nextel's transmitted power was below customary levels, the low antenna sites caused interference for other users, including public-safety land mobile-radio users, when they were close to Nextel transmitter sites.[43] In 2004, FCC, in response to input from stakeholders including Nextel and the public safety community, proposed reconfiguring the 800 MHz band to separate the two systems.[44]

Current practices and policies related to receiver performance may constrain repurposing of spectrum going forward. Representatives from three industry associations told us that it is difficult to build receivers to accommodate an unknown future. As one industry association member told us, the problem is not a lack of information on the current environment but a lack of predictability about the future environment. To make meaningful decisions about current receiver performance, the future use of spectrum would need to be better defined. FCC's TAC stated that part of the problem of increased receiver interference was the result of receivers having been built without adequate knowledge of future

---

[42]See *In the Matter of Amendment of Part 27 of the Commission's Rules to Govern the Operation of Wireless Communications Services in the 2.3 GHz Band*, 25 FCC Rcd. 11,710 (2010).

[43]Summary based on Pierre de Vries, *Radio Regulation Summit: Defining Inter-channel Operating Rules*, A report on a Silicon Flatirons Summit on Information Policy (Dec. 2, 2009).

[44]*In the Matter of Improving Public Safety in the 800MHz Band*, Report and Order, 19 FCC Rcd. 14,969, 19 FCC Rcd. 19,651, 19 FCC Rcd. 21,818 (2004).

environmental performance constraints. Moreover, several stakeholders we interviewed also said that it would be difficult and could take considerable time to upgrade or replace receivers and equipment currently in use once deployed. In November 2012, an FCC official also testified that receiver performance is increasingly becoming a limiting factor in the repurposing of spectrum for new uses and in packing services closer together, and the official said that a continuing challenge for FCC will be to maximize the amount of usable spectrum for cost effective deployment of new communication services while sufficiently protecting incumbent receivers.[45] FCC officials also said that interference problems between adjacent bands are growing and are more common in rulemakings; as noted in a recent proceeding on wireless innovation and investment, FCC stated that these rulemakings can be protracted, create uncertainty, and discourage investment.[46]

Stakeholders and Reports Identified Standards, Interference Limits, and Other Options to Improve Receiver Performance

Given the challenges that exist to improving receiver performance, stakeholders we interviewed identified options that could be taken or led by FCC and NTIA, with the aim of increasing spectrum efficiency. Below we list several recurring options based on our interviews with industry associations, manufacturers and commercial licensees, federal agencies, and representatives from academia and research organizations, as well as our review of reports from federal advisory committees and workshops on this topic (see table 1). This list of options is not exhaustive, but provides information on options that could be implemented alone or in combination. Moreover, the options could be applied to varying degrees; that is, applied to specific spectrum uses or boundaries between two different uses or on a wider scale. In fact, many stakeholders we interviewed indicated that each case of adjacent-band interference is unique, so a one-size-fits-all solution is likely not desirable or possible.

Each of the options listed below entail advantages and disadvantages, as identified by stakeholders and reports, and thus implementing any of

---

[45]Statement of Ronald T. Repasi, Deputy Chief, Office of Engineering and Technology, Federal Communications Commission, Before the House Communications and Technology Subcommittee, Energy and Commerce Committee, U.S. House of Representatives, "The Role of Receivers in a Spectrum Scarce World." November 29, 2012.

[46]*In the Matter of Fostering Innovation and Investment in the Wireless Communications Market*, 24 FCC Rcd. 11,322, 11,332 (2009).

these options would involve trade-offs. Through our interviews, a commonly mentioned disadvantage of improving receiver performance was that receivers would cost more, as more components are used in their manufacture. In addition, many stakeholders also said that actions to upgrade or replace existing, legacy receivers could be costly or take a long time, particularly in the case of equipment designed to last for many years. Stakeholders frequently stated that an advantage of improving receiver performance was increased spectrum efficiency. It is difficult to quantify or estimate the overall costs and benefits of improving receiver performance or the amount of spectrum to be gained through improving receiver performance, especially given the numerous and varied uses of spectrum. FCC, NTIA, and others have studied many of these options, and at a conceptual level, the advantages and disadvantages are well known. However, some of these options have not been implemented, while others have only been implemented in limited cases. Therefore, the practical effects of each option, that is, what *would* happen if the option is implemented, are not well known. Many of the stakeholders we interviewed indicated that receiver performance is an important aspect of spectrum efficiency, so that it warrants further consideration as spectrum management agencies and spectrum users look for ways to make more efficient use of spectrum. For example, a group of experts convened by the Silicon Flatirons Center agreed that the advance of wireless technologies and maturing infrastructures had reached an inflection point where past methods of governance were no longer adequate and generally supported that spectrum management agencies more explicitly consider receivers when drafting rules.[47]

---

[47]Pierre de Vries, *Radio Regulation Summit: Defining Inter-channel Operating Rules*, A report on a Silicon Flatirons Summit on Information Policy, held September 8-9, 2009 (Dec. 2, 2009).

Table 1: Options Identified by Stakeholders and Reports to Improve Receiver Performance

Options	Description	Advantages	Disadvantages
Greater use of industry-developed standards			
• **Voluntary, industry standards** (status quo for commercial spectrum users)	Standards-setting bodies and industry groups develop voluntary standards, which can include parameters to help prevent interference from adjacent spectrum users.	• Viewed by some as successful in mitigating interference. • Less likely to fall behind industry change or slow innovation compared to mandatory standards.	• May not be used by manufacturers and licensees. • Viewed by some as insufficient to date to incent licensees and manufacturers to improve receiver performance.
• **Safe harbor**	Compliance with industry standards would be a prerequisite to claim harmful interference, so spectrum users that do not meet standards would not be entitled to interference protection from spectrum management agencies.	• Less likely to fall behind industry change or slow innovation compared to mandated standards. • Allows manufacturers flexibility in choosing to comply or not.	• Some lower-performing receivers would not be entitled to protection, which could be difficult in the case of widely deployed consumer devices.
• **Mandatory standards** (status quo for many federal spectrum users)	Receiver standards would be mandatory, likely through regulation.	• Easy to implement compared to other approaches, as it can be verified through testing. • Approach is already widely used by NTIA. • Viewed by some as successful in mitigating interference.	• Mandated standards, if set by FCC or NTIA, could potentially slow innovation. • Raises questions about FCC's authority to broadly regulate receivers.
Interference limits	This approach would explicitly set the level of interfering signals that a receiver would have to tolerate before making a claim of harmful interference.	• Provides spectrum users with greater certainty by setting a criterion for claiming harmful interference. • Could help enable private negotiation to resolve interference. • Does not mandate a specific technology or design.	• Complex to develop and enforce, compared to standards. • Untested approach.
Additional information on spectrum use	Make additional information available on spectrum use and the characteristics of systems, including receivers.	• Enables more informed decision-making by spectrum managers and users. • Helps new entrants better understand the potential for interference. • Quick to implement compared to other approaches.	• Raises concerns about improper disclosure of proprietary and classified information. • Though quick to implement, requires resources to implement and maintain. • May be insufficient on its own to improve receiver performance.
Research and development	Promote research and development on receiver technologies and modeling.	• Provide more accurate information on current and prospective receiver performance. • Could help enable improvements to receivers and help lower cost of high-performing receivers.	• Advances in receiver technologies, particularly filters, may not be widely applicable. • Federal government may lack infrastructure to directly support research.

Source: GAO analysis of interviews and reports.

Greater Use of Industry-Developed Standards

Many stakeholders we interviewed and reports we reviewed stated that greater use of industry standards could take different forms. Use of standards, voluntary and mandatory, has been long discussed and is widely understood since standards are currently used by nonfederal and federal spectrum users to varying degrees. For instance, NTIA has mandated use of industry standards for receivers for many federal spectrum uses, as noted earlier. Stakeholders offered three main ways that industry-developed standards could be used: voluntary, a safe harbor allowing spectrum users that meet standards to receive protection from harmful interference, and mandatory, all described in greater detail in table 1.

Stakeholders we interviewed varied in their support for these options, but many opposed mandatory standards. Many stakeholders told us they prefer the industry-led, voluntary standard-creating process, in contrast to government-created and mandated standards, as they believe industry-developed voluntary standards can be responsive and flexible to changing conditions. While mandatory standards were often opposed as an overall option to improve receiver performance, some stakeholders told us mandatory standards could be used in limited cases, such as when market forces do not sufficiently incentivize the production of robust receivers or when receivers are not tied to the licensee (i.e., decoupled receivers). For the safe harbor option, whereby compliance with extant industry standards would serve as a prerequisite for receiving protection from interference, several industry associations and individual stakeholders we spoke with supported this option. In 2003, NTIA recommended that FCC adopt industry standards on a voluntary or recommended basis, with FCC only granting protection for services with receivers that meet standards, and in doing so, NTIA suggested that FCC give priority to bands being reallocated to avoid problems encountered with legacy systems.[48] In addition, federal programs have encouraged compliance with industry standards among nonfederal spectrum users through grants or other funding. For example, the Department of Homeland Security's Emergency Communications Grant program requires that funds used by public safety agencies to purchase land mobile radio systems comply with industry standards set by TIA. As part of the transition from analog to digital television, NTIA offered coupons to

---

[48]*NTIA Comments on Interference Immunity Performance Specifications for Radio Receivers* (Washington, D.C.: Nov. 12, 2003).

subsidize consumer purchases of converter boxes, but the coupons could only be used to purchase converter boxes that met minimum performance standards.[49]

Regardless of the form of standards used, there are some overarching advantages and disadvantages. Advantages of greater use of industry-developed standards are that this option makes use of existing standards and that the open, consensus-based process used to develop most industry standards helps ensure they reflect the knowledge and input of a range of industry and government perspectives. Disadvantages are that standards may not keep pace with industry change and can be prescriptive, limiting flexibility of manufacturers and licensees. Also, industry standards do not exist for all services. Further, as discussed earlier, industry standards tend to focus within a band or service rather than looking across boundaries; however, a few stakeholders we interviewed said FCC or NTIA could encourage standards-settings bodies to address particular problems, such as interference, or encourage more cross-industry bodies to help enhance industry standards. Some additional advantages and disadvantages apply to different forms of greater use of industry-developed standards, as listed in table 1.

Interference Limits

Another option identified by stakeholders we interviewed and cited by reports was interference limits. The interference limits approach would explicitly set the level of energy—that is, the strength of the unwanted signal from adjacent bands—that a receiver would have to tolerate before making a claim of harmful interference. This is in contrast to the current situation where expectations of receiver performance have almost always been implicit—that is, receivers have been expected to operate within the same parameters as their associated transmitters—which can lead to conflicts when parties have a different understanding of these expectations.[50] Interference limits differ from the safe-harbor standards

---

[49]*Rules to Implement and Administer a Coupon Program for Digital-to-Analog Converter Boxes*, 72 Fed. Reg. 12,097, 12,101 (Mar. 15, 2007). Converter boxes allowed consumers with analog televisions to continue to be able to receive over-the-air television signals after the broadcasters switched to all digital broadcasts.

[50]For more information, see Federal Communications Commission, Technological Advisory Council, Receivers and Spectrum Working Group, *Interference Limits Policy: The use of harm claim thresholds to improve the interference tolerance of wireless systems*, White Paper (Feb. 6, 2013), accessed Feb. 13, 2013, http://transition.fcc.gov/bureaus/oet/tac/tacdocs/WhitePaperTACInterferenceLimitsv1.0.pdf

option discussed above, since under the interference limits approach, the prerequisite for claiming harmful interference is demonstrating that the level of energy the receiver is exposed to exceeds a predetermined level, rather than demonstrating a receiver complies with industry standards, typically stated as specific performance characteristics.

Recently, reports from both a working group within FCC's TAC and PCAST recommended that FCC test interference limits. The TAC working group recommended that FCC identify one or more pieces of spectrum, specifically adjacent spectrum allocations, that are good candidates for interference limits and initiate multi-stakeholder groups of relevant industry and government representatives to work out issues and implementation choices for these pieces of spectrum. PCAST recommended that NTIA and FCC take steps to consider both transmitters and receivers in its spectrum management policies and specified that an initial step should be trying interference limits. Other approaches to interference rights have been proposed, including one that aims to replace FCC's current policy of first-in-time rights—whereby FCC protects incumbent users and thus receivers from interference as a result of rule changes—to a policy where users would have to self-protect against interference in adjacent bands.[51]

The advantages of this option cited by stakeholders and reports that we reviewed are that it would provide spectrum users with greater certainty, as it sets a criterion for harmful interference. In addition, this option could help enable private negotiation rather than FCC involvement to resolve potential and realized interference. Another advantage is that this option does not mandate a specific technology or design, leaving such choices to manufacturers and others. Among the disadvantages cited by stakeholders and reports are that this option would be more complex to develop and enforce compared to standards. Also, this option has not been used or tested, so it could take considerable time and resources to

---

[51]For more information on this approach, see Evan Kwerel and John Williams, "Forward-Looking Interference Regulation," *The Unfinished Radio Revolution: Eight Perspectives on Wireless Interference*, ed. Pierre de Vries and Kaleb A. Sieh, vol. 9 of *Journal on Telecommunications and High Technology Law* (Boulder, CO: Spring 2011), 516.

test and considerable time to implement and the practical effects and outcomes are unknown.[52]

Additional Information on Spectrum Use

Many stakeholders we interviewed said that additional transparency and sharing of information on spectrum use and system characteristics by FCC and NTIA could help mitigate interference problems involving receivers by facilitating greater understanding of the systems already in place and thus the potential for interference to arise from the deployment of a new system in adjacent spectrum. In general, stakeholders identified two ways that additional information could be made available.

- First, FCC and NTIA could make more information available on the characteristics of transmitters and receivers in use, potentially in conjunction with a spectrum inventory.[53] The CSMAC Interference and Dynamic Spectrum Access Subcommittee recommended that NTIA, FCC, or other government entities responsible for managing spectrum establish a clearinghouse to make information available to those seeking to obtain access to spectrum; this will give entities considering new services visibility about the potential for interference for such equipment before they acquire spectrum and deploy equipment.[54] NTIA said that resources for implementing this and other CSMAC recommendations were not included in recent budgets, but some of its ongoing band-specific and other initiatives correspond with these recommendations.

- Second, FCC could also compile and share information on existing industry standards for receivers. The TAC working group on receivers

---

[52]In the United Kingdom, Ofcom officials said that spectrum usage rights—an approach akin with those described above—have been implemented for one band; but, spectrum usage rights have not been more widely adopted or tested to date.

[53]Legislation was introduced in the 112th Congress to address the lack of publicly available data on spectrum usage. Reforming Airwaves by Developing Incentives and Opportunistic Sharing Act, S. 455, § 3, 112th Cong. (2011). The bill would have required FCC to prepare an inventory of radio spectrum bands managed by FCC, including the number of transmitters and receiver terminals in use and information on receiver performance.

[54]This report included several recommendations to NTIA, FCC, and any other government entities responsible for spectrum management related to making information available on spectrum use and characteristics. See CSMAC, *Interference and Dynamic Spectrum Access Subcommittee Final Report*.

and spectrum found that industry and government receiver standards and recommended practices may exist but are often unknown to manufacturers and users operating in adjacent bands. Therefore, the TAC working group recommended that FCC enhance its Spectrum Dashboard—a tool on FCC's website that provides information on how different frequency bands are being used and allows the public to search, map, and download data on licenses—to include receiver standards.

In terms of advantages, making additional information available would enable more informed decision-making by NTIA, FCC, and spectrum users through enhanced planning and testing. Moreover, additional information could help new entrants better understand the spectrum environment and potential interference concerns before committing resources; as part of its report, the CSMAC Interference and Dynamic Spectrum Access Subcommittee stated that some of the interference problems in recent years were not anticipated by new entrants and might have been avoided by providing new entrants with the interference characteristics of receiving and transmitting equipment used in adjacent bands. FCC and NTIA could also take action on this option quickly, compared to other options. However, several stakeholders said that concerns about proprietary and classified information could make it difficult to implement this option. In addition, it would require resources, both from federal spectrum management agencies and spectrum users, to implement this option and keep it up to date. Finally, making additional information on spectrum use available may be insufficient on its own to address the challenges to improving receiver performance.

Research and Development

To improve receiver performance and increase spectrum efficiency, the federal government could promote research and development for receiver technologies and modeling. FCC officials told us that not much is known about the actual performance of receivers. A 2010 report prepared by the CSMAC Interference and Dynamic Spectrum Access Subcommittee found that more research is needed to evaluate advances in technologies and what standards will yield more spectrally efficient equipment, since such advances may significantly alter cost-performance trade-offs. More specifically, it recommended that the federal government could fund research to accelerate the development of filters to improve the performance of receivers, such as the ability to reject an undesired signal at frequencies close to the desired signal frequency, without affecting size or power consumption. The report also noted that a better dialogue between the filter community and spectrum managers is essential as filter performance has a large impact on spectrum efficiency. One licensee we interviewed said that more investment is needed to improve technology for receivers and that new technology could help lower the cost and increase the flexibility of devices. A group like the Wireless Spectrum Research and Development's Senior Steering Group could be used to help coordinate research in this area across the federal government.[55] Additional information gleaned through research could enable spectrum managers and users to better understand the current state of receiver performance and help inform future choices.

Stakeholders said that an advantage of research and development would be to provide FCC and NTIA with more accurate information on interference mitigation technologies that are feasible. Stakeholders said that research could also help enable improvements to receivers to help prevent interference problems across bands. Conversely, this option would require resources, not only to fund but also to coordinate research efforts across the federal government and the private sector. Also, certain advancements through research, like those in filtering, may not be applicable across spectrum uses. A few members from one industry association we interviewed also said that filters can help solve some but not all problems of adjacent band interference. Finally, the federal government may lack infrastructure (e.g., test bed, labs) to directly support research.

Conclusions

As demand for and use of spectrum continues to increase, improving the performance of receivers is one of several ways to more efficiently use spectrum and accommodate new services. To date, there have been a limited number of instances where interference concerns driven by receiver performance have impeded a licensee's planned use of adjacent spectrum. Even so, PCAST and FCC, among others, have recognized the growing impact of receivers on efficient spectrum use, and adjacent-band interference concerns may increase in years to come as spectrum management agencies look to allocate additional spectrum for wireless broadband and other new services in an already crowded environment.

---

[55]Formed as result of a 2010 Presidential Memorandum, *Unleashing the Wireless Broadband Revolution*, the Wireless Spectrum Research and Development's Senior Steering Group coordinates spectrum-related research and development activities across the federal government, and helps identify gaps in the government's research and development portfolio with respect to spectrally efficient technologies.

Therefore, many stakeholders feel that more can and should be done to improve receiver performance in concert with other efforts to increase spectrum efficiency—the status quo is increasingly becoming untenable. Stakeholders have identified and studied several options to improve receiver performance and the efficient use of spectrum. In some instances, these options entail direct federal intervention, such as imposing mandatory standards for receivers, whereas in others, federal policy creates an environment where industry participants' individual and collective actions can improve receiver performance. Each of these options entail advantages, including reduced actual and potential interference and improved spectrum efficiency, and disadvantages, including possibly higher equipment costs. FCC and NTIA have each explored receiver performance in the past, and recent recommendations from advisory committees specific to this topic provide Congress, NTIA and FCC, and industry stakeholders with options for further consideration and testing. Since the topic has been the subject of considerable study, the potential advantages and disadvantages of various options are generally understood. However, less is known about the practical effects of implementing these options to address interference. Several options have not been implemented, such as safe harbor standards and interference limits, and others, such as mandatory standards, have only been implemented for certain federal users, and it is unclear how these experiences would translate to nonfederal users. Greater understanding of the practical effects of these options will allow FCC to make more informed spectrum-management decisions moving forward to ensure the efficient and effective use of spectrum.

Recommendation for Executive Action

To improve receiver performance and spectrum efficiency, we recommend that the Chairman of the Federal Communications Commission consider collecting information on the practical effects of various options to improve receiver performance, including consideration of small-scale pilot tests of these options.

Agency Comments and Our Evaluation

We provided a draft of this report to the Department of Commerce (Commerce) and FCC for review and comment. In response to the draft report, Commerce and FCC provided written comments, which are reprinted in appendixes II and III, respectively. In its letter, Commerce said that it will continue to work with FCC on issues of potential interference. Commerce also emphasized the federal government's use of standards to improve receiver performance and the benefits of receiver performance characteristics as a factor in improving spectrum efficiency. In its letter, FCC said that the Commission has already initiated a process to gather information on the effects of options to improve receiver performance; FCC discussed various actions under way, which we describe in this report, including that FCC's TAC recently submitted to the Commission for consideration recommendations to improve receiver performance. These actions will help FCC to understand the potential advantages and disadvantages of various options to improve receiver performance. However, we do not believe that these actions will provide information on the practical effects of options that FCC might get from a pilot test or other information-collection efforts, which, as we note in the report, will allow FCC to make more informed spectrum-management decisions. Commerce and FCC also provided technical corrections to the draft report that we incorporated as appropriate.

We are sending copies of this report to the Secretary of Commerce, the Chairman of the Federal Communications Commission, and the appropriate congressional committees. In addition, the report will be available at no charge on GAO's website at http://www.gao.gov.

If you or members of your staff have any questions about this report, please contact me at (202) 512-2834 or goldsteinm@gao.gov. Contact points for our Offices of Congressional Relations and Public Affairs may be found on the last page of this report. Major contributors to this report are listed in appendix IV.

Mark L. Goldstein
Director
Physical Infrastructure Issues

Appendix I: Objectives, Scope, and Methodology

This report examines efforts by commercial licensees, manufacturers, and the federal government to ensure that transmission systems are designed and operated so as to not compromise reasonable use of adjacent spectrum, with a focus on receiver performance as it relates to increasing the efficient use of spectrum. In particular, the report provides information on (1) actions taken by selected manufacturers and commercial licensees to improve receiver performance; (2) actions taken by the federal government to improve receiver performance; (3) challenges, if any, to improving receiver performance; and (4) options identified by stakeholders and reports to improve receiver performance.

Scope and Methodology

To address the engagement's objectives, we reviewed relevant statutes and regulations, and Federal Communications Commission (FCC) and National Telecommunications and Information Administration (NTIA) documents related to spectrum management, interference, and transmission systems, with a focus on receivers. FCC and NTIA documents included presentations from FCC's March 2012 workshop on Spectrum Efficiency and Receiver Performance and NTIA's *Receiver Spectrum Standards Phase 1–Summary of Research into Existing Standards*, as well as various notices, orders, advisory committee reports, and other publications. We interviewed FCC and NTIA officials to learn about actions the spectrum management agencies have taken to improve receiver performance, with a focus on interference between adjacent spectrum users, and reviewed reports and workshops held by the agencies on the topic of receiver performance. We also interviewed members of NTIA's Interdepartment Radio Advisory Committee (IRAC), which consists of representatives from federal departments and agencies, and officials from the National Oceanic and Atmospheric Administration (NOAA) to learn about federal spectrum users' experiences with adjacent-band interference and actions to improve receiver performance to increase spectrum efficiency.

We also interviewed a variety of other stakeholders outside the federal government—specifically industry associations, commercial licensees and manufacturers, and academics and representatives from research organizations—to learn about receiver performance and spectrum efficiency. We selected industry associations to cover a variety of spectrum uses and provide the perspectives of both licensees and manufacturers. We selected commercial licensees and manufacturers to ensure variety in frequency and application and to correspond to interference cases involving receiver concerns. We selected academics and representatives from research organizations based on participation in workshops on receiver performance, service on FCC or NTIA advisory committees, and recommendations from other interviewees, among other criteria. In addition, we interviewed officials from spectrum management agencies in Canada and the United Kingdom to learn about steps taken in those countries to improve receiver performance to increase spectrum efficiency. Across these interviews, we discussed the advantages and disadvantages of improving receiver performance to increase spectrum efficiency; actions taken by the commercial licensees, manufacturers, and the federal government to improve receiver performance; and options for additional action to improve receiver performance.

Table 2 provides a complete list of those we interviewed for this report. The information and perspectives that we obtained from the interviews may not be generalized to all industry stakeholders that have an interest in spectrum efficiency and receiver performance. Rather, comments and views are reviewed in context with current literature on this topic.

Table 2: Organizations and Individuals Interviewed

Industry associations
Association of Public-Safety Communications Officials
Consumer Electronics Association
CTIA - The Wireless Association
International Wireless Industry Consortium
National Association of Broadcasters
National Cable and Telecommunications Association
National Public Safety Telecommunications Council
National Spectrum Management Association
RTCA, Inc.
Rural Carriers Association
Satellite Industry Association
Telecommunications Industry Association
Wireless Internet Service Providers Association
Commercial licensees and manufacturers
AT&T
Garmin International
John Deere
LightSquared
Motorola
Sprint
Trimble

Academics, representatives from research organizations, and consultants
Dale Hatfield, Silicon Flatirons Center
Dennis Roberson, Illinois Institute of Technology
Harold Feld, Public Knowledge
Evan Kwerel, FCC,[a] and John Williams, Ambit
Michael Calabrese, New America Foundation
Michael Marcus, Marcus Spectrum Solutions LLC
Paul Kolodzy, Kolodzy Consulting LLC
Paul Sinderbrand, WCS Coalition Legal Counsel
Pierre de Vries, Silicon Flatirons Center
William Webb, Neul
Spectrum management agencies
Industry Canada
Ofcom – United Kingdom regulator

Source: GAO.

[a]We included Evan Kwerel of FCC in this table since he was identified based on our criteria for
selecting academics and representatives from research organizations to interview.

We also analyzed literature on receiver performance, standards, and
interference from academic journals as well as workshop proceedings
and reports on receiver performance and interference conducted by FCC,
NTIA, and organizations like the Silicon Flatirons Center, Brookings
Institution, and Aspen Institute. To identify relevant literature, we
performed a search of papers and studies (from 2002 through 2012) from
major electronic databases, such as ProQuest and SciSearch. We
included studies that focused on interference between adjacent spectrum
users and spectrum efficiency. We only included papers from scholarly
peer-reviewed journals, government reports, conference papers, and
other working papers. We also conducted a targeted search for
proceedings from conferences that occurred between 2008 and 2012 that
covered receiver performance, spectrum, and interference. We reviewed
the relevant papers, studies, and conference proceedings to identify
options to improve receiver performance as well as the advantages and
disadvantages of taking action to improve receiver performance.

We also studied a judgmental sample of cases where receiver
performance played a role in cases of potential or realized interference
between adjacent spectrum users, to better understand the actions of
commercial licensees, manufacturers, and the federal government as well
as the trade-offs of solutions sought in each case. We selected cases to
ensure variation in application or use (e.g., cellular telephone, navigation),
federal and nonfederal users, and existence of receiver standards, among
other characteristics. To compile a list of possible cases, we reviewed

FCC and NTIA reports, including the FCC's Technological Advisory
Council white paper on spectrum efficiency metrics that included an
appendix on receiver performance and NTIA published reports on
interference involving federal users, and discussed potential cases with
officials from FCC and NTIA. We selected two cases that primarily
involved nonfederal spectrum users: (1) interference between cellular and
public safety services in the 800 MHz band, and (2) potential interference
between satellite radio and wireless communication in the 2.3 GHz band.
We sought to select a third case of interference involving federal
spectrum users of radar systems. However, since our aim was to select
cases that involved receiver performance problems, and since NTIA
officials told us that many cases of interference involving federal spectrum
users are resolved without substantial NTIA involvement, we did not
select a particular interference case. Rather, we chose to study radar
systems more generally. For each case, we analyzed relevant rulemaking
proceedings, reports, and other documents to describe the types and
extent of actions taken by stakeholders to limit interference and increase
spectrum efficiency. In addition, we interviewed select licensees, industry
associations, and manufacturers to better understand the circumstances
of each case, actions taken to address interference, and the trade-offs of
these actions.

Case Study Descriptions

WCS/SDARS: In the 2.3 GHz band, interference concerns arose between
two different services—terrestrial-based Wireless Communications
Service (WCS) and chiefly satellite-based Satellite Digital Audio Radio
Service (SDARS, or satellite radio)—allocated to adjacent parts of the
bands with no guard bands separating the services. WCS allows a range
of terrestrial-based services, including fixed, mobile, portable, and
radiolocation services, though initial rules for the band made mobile
service impractical. SDARS is primarily a satellite-based service in which
programming is sent directly from satellites to receivers that are either at
a fixed location or in motion; however, SDARS licensees deployed
terrestrial repeaters to address situations where skyscrapers and other
impediments prevented a line-of-sight connection between satellites and
receivers. In general, SDARS receivers must be highly sensitive to
receive weak, satellite signals. Moreover, SDARS deployed before WCS,
so SDARS receivers did not have to tolerate high-powered mobile
operations in the adjacent WCS bands. SDARS licensees raised
concerns over interference from a request to change rules to enable
mobile services in the WCS spectrum, while WCS licensees and others
raised concern over potential interference from the SDARS terrestrial
repeaters.

FCC issued several notices of proposed rulemaking for both services since their allocation in the mid 1990s. FCC also encouraged the parties to negotiate an agreement to facilitate the adoption of rules for both services that would resolve the potential for interference. However, negotiations did not lead to a private resolution, and in 2007, FCC opened a new proceeding to update the record on the potential interference. This culminated in a 2010 Report and Order and Second Report and Order that adopted rules addressing the potential interference.[1] FCC adopted rules that, among other things, effectively created 5 MHz guard bands on each side of the SDARS spectrum to protect legacy SDARS receivers; the rules did not include any requirements specific to receiver performance. In 2012, FCC responded to petitions for reconsideration of that decision with a new order that adopted an agreement reached by AT&T and Sirius XM, which are now the primary license holders in the band.[2]

800 MHz band: Interference occurred between adjacent spectrum users in the 800 MHz band primarily because of the use of two different types of communications systems on interleaved channels. The two types of communications systems were (1) cellular-architecture multi-cell systems used by cellular telephone and enhanced specialized mobile radios and (2) high site systems used by public safety and well as private wireless and non-cellular specialized mobile radio licensees. Beyond the difference in systems, two other factors exacerbated the potential for interference: the close proximity of frequencies used by the commercial and public safety users and insufficient selectivity of many land mobile radios used by public safety users.

Interference from cellular systems to public safety systems began to occur in the late 1990s as cellular licensees began deploying multi-cell systems. Interference occurred even though all the licensees were operating in compliance with FCC rules for transmitters. After interference problems emerged, FCC brought together the relevant parties and encouraged them to develop more definitive information on the scope and

---

[1] *In the Matter of Amendment of Part 27 of the Commission's Rules to Govern the Operation of Wireless Communications Services in the 2.3 GHZ Band*, 25 FCC Rcd. 11,710 (2010).

[2] *In the Matter of Amendment of Part 27 of the Commission's Rules to Govern the Operation of Wireless Communications Services in the 2.3 GHZ Band*, 27 FCC Rcd. 13,651 (2012).

severity of the problem and to recommend steps to mitigate interference. As a result, a working group created a Best Practices Guide to help prevent and mitigate interference in the band. Seeking a more comprehensive solution to the interference problem, Nextel—the primary license holder in the 800 MHz band—proposed reconfiguring the band to separate the different systems and then worked with many public safety and other industry associations to create an updated reconfiguration plan. In addition, the public safety community and equipment manufacturers recommended receiver performance specifications going forward that would serve as criteria for qualifying for interference protection. FCC adopted these recommendations in the rules it adopted for the 800 MHz band in 2004, which reconfigured the band and defined a technical standard for determining if a public safety or other non-cellular licensee is entitled to interference protection.[3]

---

[3]See *In the Matter of Improving Public Safety in the 800MHz Band*, 19 FCC Rcd. 14,969, 14,973, *Second Erratum*, 19 FCC Rcd. 19,651, *Third Erratum*, 19 FCC Rcd. 21,818 (2004).

Appendix II: Comments from the Department of Commerce

UNITED STATES DEPARTMENT OF COMMERCE
The Assistant Secretary for Communications
and Information
Washington, D.C. 20230

FEB 6 2013

The Honorable Gene L. Dodaro
Comptroller General
U.S. Government Accountability Office
441 G Street, NW
Washington, DC 20548

Dear Comptroller General Dodaro:

Thank you for the opportunity to review and comment on the U.S. Government Accountability Office's (GAO) draft report entitled *Spectrum Management: Further Consideration of Options to Improve Receiver Performance Needed* (GAO-13-265). The National Telecommunications and Information Administration (NTIA) appreciates the work that GAO has done to highlight the actions NTIA has taken to improve receiver performance. NTIA recognizes the benefits of receiver performance characteristics as a factor in improving the efficiency and effectiveness of spectrum management and concurs with the draft report's findings.

As discussed in the Report, the federal government uses standards to improve receiver performance. For example, NTIA mandated receiver standards for land mobile radio, fixed, and radar systems. The Federal Aviation Administration publishes Technical Standard Orders that refer to Radio Technical Commission for Aeronautics standards for aviation receivers. The United States Coast Guard uses maritime receiver standards developed by the International Electrotechnical Commission. The Inter-Range Instrumentation Group developed receiver standards for aeronautical telemetry systems. NTIA also requires compliance with industry-developed transmitter and receiver standards where applicable.

NTIA will continue to work closely with the Federal Communications Commission (FCC) on particular service or band-specific proceedings in which issues arise regarding potential out-of-band and adjacent band interference between federal and non-federal systems. Through the notice and comment rulemaking process, or in pre-rulemaking collaborative efforts such as those now taking place in the Commerce Spectrum Management Advisory Committee, interested parties can be made aware of the performance characteristics of proposed and existing receiving and transmitting equipment on a case-by-case basis, which will better inform the FCC's proceedings.

Thank you again for the opportunity to review and comment on the draft report.

Sincerely,

Lawrence E. Strickling

Appendix III: Comments from the Federal Communications Commission

Federal Communications Commission
Washington, D.C. 20554

February 8, 2013

Mr. Gene L. Dodaro
Comptroller General
Government Accountability Office
441 G Street, NW
Washington, DC 20548

Dear Mr. Dodaro:

Thank you for the opportunity to review and comment on the Government Accountability Office's (GAO) draft report, entitled Spectrum Management: Further Consideration of Options to Improve Receive Performance Needed. In your draft report, you recommend that, to improve receiver performance and efficiency, the FCC consider collecting data on the practical effect of various options to improve receiver performance. The FCC has already initiated this type of fact-gathering process.

Receiver performance is an area of increased attention as the Commission seeks to make more efficient use of the radio frequency spectrum. Last year, Chairman Genachowski initiated a review of spectrum efficiency and receiver standards with a two-day workshop held at FCC headquarters featuring a broad range of experts and stakeholders, including licensees, equipment manufacturers, and consumers. Commission staff also regularly participates in various technical groups organized by private sector entities to discuss ideas about how to address receiver spectrum issues and meets with filter and electronic component suppliers to discuss technology developments that hold promise for improving the interference rejection capabilities of receivers. Moreover, Chairman Genachowski tasked the Commission's Technological Advisory Council (TAC) to study the issue of receiver performance.

The Receivers and Spectrum Work Group of the TAC addressed the role of receivers in ensuring efficient use of the spectrum while avoiding potential obstacles to making spectrum available for new services. The TAC Work Group concluded generally that the private sector has published receiver standards for many services, but they often are not developed in coordination with adjacent services, are not well known, and their basis is not well understood. The Work Group also introduced a new and novel approach to incentivize improved receiver performance. The new approach would establish an interference protection limit between services to define the signal levels that the services would be expected to tolerate from adjacent services. Service providers and equipment manufacturers would then have the information they need to design their equipment to tolerate these signal levels. A licensee would need to demonstrate that it is experiencing signal levels above the limit in order to make a claim of harmful interference (harm claim threshold).

In December 2012, the TAC submitted to the Commission for consideration recommendations to improve receiver performance. The recommendations include: 1] Implementing a web-accessible receiver standards & voluntary receiver specification repository through the FCC Dashboard; 2] Fostering

Multi-Stakeholder (MSH) Group(s) to consider an interference limits policy at one or more service boundaries, including current/future receiver performance levels; 3) Issuing appropriate requests for information on an interference limits policy focusing on current bands of interest; and 4) Establishing a focused effort to develop the needed technical foundation to support the establishment of harm claim thresholds. The TAC is also on schedule to release by the end of this month its White Paper on Interference Limits Policy recommendations and the use of harm claim thresholds to improve the interference tolerance of wireless systems.

Receiver performance is becoming increasingly important as a limiting factor as the Commission moves to repurpose spectrum and pack more services closer together. The continuing challenge will be to maximize the amount of useable spectrum for cost-effective deployment of new communication services while sufficiently protecting incumbent receivers. If receiver technology remains static or is unable to keep pace with the rapid evolution of the transmission technologies, the challenges before the Commission will increase dramatically.

The Commission has and will continue to collaborate with NTIA to make available a total of 500 MHz of additional federal and non-federal spectrum suitable for both mobile and fixed wireless broadband use by 2020. To do this, the Commission is focusing on complementary approaches including: auctioning additional spectrum, removing regulatory barriers to flexible spectrum use, clearing new bands for flexible broadband use and promoting advanced spectrum sharing techniques. Since the large majority of spectrum is shared among commercial and federal users, implementing any approach to make additional spectrum available for mobile broadband will result in frequency adjacencies to federal users. Therefore a comprehensive approach between the FCC and NTIA will be needed to incorporate receiver performance into our collective spectrum management responsibilities that involves both non-federal and federal spectrum users.

We are committed to maximizing efficient use of the spectrum including taking steps to improve receiver performance. To achieve these goals, the Commission will need to consider whether the approach recommended by the TAC, other approaches, or a combination of approaches may be the best way forward. There are many factors to consider such as their effectiveness, viability and costs compared to benefits, among others and further work that may need to be completed. Moreover, we will continue to work closely with NTIA and other federal stakeholders as we consider next steps.

Sincerely,

Julius P. Knapp
Chief
Office of Engineering and Technology
Federal Communications Commission

Appendix IV: GAO Contact and Staff Acknowledgments

GAO Contact	Mark L. Goldstein, (202) 512-2834 or goldsteinm@gao.gov
Staff Acknowledgments	In addition to the contact person named above, Michael Clements, Assistant Director; Nabajyoti Barkakati; Stephen Brown; Leia Dickerson; Sharon Dyer; Ryan Eisner; David Goldstein; Richard Hung; Bert Japikse; Joanie Lofgren; Maren McAvoy; Joshua Ormond; Amy Rosewarne; Hai Tran; Elizabeth Wood; and Nancy Zearfoss made key contributions to this report.

GAO's Mission	The Government Accountability Office, the audit, evaluation, and investigative arm of Congress, exists to support Congress in meeting its constitutional responsibilities and to help improve the performance and accountability of the federal government for the American people. GAO examines the use of public funds; evaluates federal programs and policies; and provides analyses, recommendations, and other assistance to help Congress make informed oversight, policy, and funding decisions. GAO's commitment to good government is reflected in its core values of accountability, integrity, and reliability.
Obtaining Copies of GAO Reports and Testimony	The fastest and easiest way to obtain copies of GAO documents at no cost is through GAO's website (http://www.gao.gov). Each weekday afternoon, GAO posts on its website newly released reports, testimony, and correspondence. To have GAO e-mail you a list of newly posted products, go to http://www.gao.gov and select "E-mail Updates."
Order by Phone	The price of each GAO publication reflects GAO's actual cost of production and distribution and depends on the number of pages in the publication and whether the publication is printed in color or black and white. Pricing and ordering information is posted on GAO's website, http://www.gao.gov/ordering.htm. Place orders by calling (202) 512-6000, toll free (866) 801-7077, or TDD (202) 512-2537. Orders may be paid for using American Express, Discover Card, MasterCard, Visa, check, or money order. Call for additional information.
Connect with GAO	Connect with GAO on Facebook, Flickr, Twitter, and YouTube. Subscribe to our RSS Feeds or E-mail Updates. Listen to our Podcasts. Visit GAO on the web at www.gao.gov.
To Report Fraud, Waste, and Abuse in Federal Programs	Contact: Website: http://www.gao.gov/fraudnet/fraudnet.htm E-mail: fraudnet@gao.gov Automated answering system: (800) 424-5454 or (202) 512-7470
Congressional Relations	Katherine Siggerud, Managing Director, siggerudk@gao.gov, (202) 512-4400, U.S. Government Accountability Office, 441 G Street NW, Room 7125, Washington, DC 20548
Public Affairs	Chuck Young, Managing Director, youngc1@gao.gov, (202) 512-4800 U.S. Government Accountability Office, 441 G Street NW, Room 7149 Washington, DC 20548

Please Print on Recycled Paper.

www.ingramcontent.com/pod-product-compliance
Lightning Source LLC
Chambersburg PA
CBHW080611290526

45790CB00007B/2734